Civil War Pictures

By

D. L. CORBITT

AND

ELIZABETH W. WILBORN

Raleigh:
Division of Archives and History
North Carolina Department of Cultural Resources

Eleventh Printing, 1991

ISBN 0-86526-074-5

FOREWORD

Pictures of the Civil War Period in North Carolina was first published by the State Department of Archives and History in 1958. The pamphlet was revised and issued under the title *Civil War Pictures* in 1964. Because of the pamphlet's continuing popularity, the Historical Publications Section of the Division of Archives and History, North Carolina Department of Cultural Resources, has kept the title in print without further revision. Modernization of spelling and capitalization, the inclusion of more recent historical scholarship and interpretation, and additional illustrations would be desirable. But rather than allow popular titles such as *Civil War Pictures* to go out of print, the Historical Publications Section is reprinting older publications with minimum revisions. This eleventh printing of *Civil War Pictures* raises the number of copies of the title in print to more than 65,000. The reprint does feature a new cover, designed by Kathleen B. Wyche, an editor for the section. Robert M. Topkins, head of the General Publications Branch, saw the reprint through press.

Many of the illustrations in this pamphlet were taken from *Harper's Weekly* and *Leslie's Illustrated Weekly*. These magazines hired artists to accompany Federal forces and to make drawings of the battles, sites, and people of the war. Additional pictures were taken from *The American Soldier in the Civil War*; artifacts in the North Carolina Museum of History were photographed; and still other pictures were reproduced from the Albert Barden Collection in the Division of Archives and History.

Jeffrey J. Crow
Historical Publications Administrator

August, 1991

INTRODUCTION

The decade 1860-1870 was probably the most difficult period in American history. It was in these years that the American people fought a sectional conflict, and in many instances father fought son or brother fought brother. During this period not only was there a clash of arms which lasted four years in which thousands of soldiers were killed or wounded, but the economic life of the South was exhausted. The North suffered likewise in economic resources and man power.

The years prior to this decade had been years of discussion, conflict, and adjustment. The question of slavery and states' rights had been debated a long time in Congress and elsewhere. The extension of slavery in new territories or states was a subject of tremendous importance to the South as well as to the North. The North which had not found slaves profitable was opposed to the extension of slavery. In 1820 when the Missouri Compromise was passed in Congress, it was agreed that Missouri should join the Union as a slave state. At the same time Maine came into the Union as a free state. Thus the balance of power which was so important between the North and South was maintained. This compromise, however, did not settle the difficulties because other states soon wanted to join the Union either as free or slave states. The balance of power was ever foremost in the minds of the two sections. In 1850 another great compromise measure was passed which developed from the fact that California wanted to join the Union as a free state. As the act was finally adopted California was admitted as a free state and the territories of New Mexico and Utah based on the principle of popular sovereignty were recognized. In addition slave trade in the District of Columbia was abolished and a reduction in the size of Texas was agreed upon. An appropriation of $10,000,000 was voted to Texas theoretically as compensation for her war debt which accrued prior to 1845.

Another factor which tended to divide the North and South was the Dred Scott Decision made in 1857. In this decision the United States Supreme Court invalidated the Missouri Compromise and established the principle that Congress had no constitutional power to exclude slavery from any territory of the United States.

Of course there were other important factors, such as differences in occupations, religion, agricultural pursuits, manufacturing or the lack of it in the South, and humanitarian grounds, as well as many others.

On December 10, 1860, Bedford Brown introduced in the North Carolina Senate a resolution to send Thomas Ruffin, Weldon N. Edwards, William A. Graham, and W. N. H. Smith as commissioners to South Carolina to urge that secession be postponed until a convention of all the slaveholding states could be held. The commissioners were authorized to make the same appeal to any other state which had called for a convention.

The Committee on Federal Relations had in the meantime submitted a report in which the majority declared that the existing crisis was one of great peril to the rights and equality of the states. They recommended that a convention be called to determine the mode of redress. The minority report expressed the opinion that personal liberty laws had been standing a long time and the election of Lincoln was inadequate to justify such drastic action.

Other efforts were made to call a convention. The Union men were against the convention, but the secessionists were advocating and organizing for one.

When Abraham Lincoln was elected President in 1860, South Carolina on December 20, 1860, seceded from the Union. Mississippi (on January 9, 1861), Florida (on January 10, 1861), Georgia (on January 19, 1861), Louisiana (on January 26, 1861), and Texas (on March 2, 1861) followed in rapid succession. War-like conditions were fast developing in the South and the leaders were taking sides. The seceding states in February, 1861, formed the Confederate States of America and on March 6, established a nucleus of a regular army. Later Jefferson Davis was empowered to call for volunteers, and a Department of War came into being which aided in obtaining enlistments and also in keeping those in service who were already under arms. Plans were developed rapidly and emissaries were sent to Europe to purchase arms and supplies, and more manufacturing in the Confederacy was undertaken. The South was definitely preparing for war. It should be said that Virginia seceded April 17, 1861, and North Carolina on May 20, 1861, after President Lincoln had called for troops.

Fort Sumter located in Charleston (S. C.) harbor was held by Major Robert Anderson, who had under his command 129

Union soldiers. Earlier Anderson was also in command of Forts Johnson, Moultrie, and Castle Pinckney, but on December 20, 1860, he secretly moved all his troops to Fort Sumter. Governor Francis W. Pickens seized Fort Moultrie, Castle Pinckney, the Arsenal, and the Custom House, and demanded the immediate surrender of Anderson. President Lincoln notified Pickens and General P. G. T. Beauregard of his intention to send provisions to Anderson. Following another demand by Pickens for Anderson's surrender, Beauregard on April 12 began to bombard the Fort. This bombardment continued for two days. On April 14 Anderson capitulated.

On April 15 President Lincoln called for 75,000 troops from the states to help suppress the southern "insurrection." North Carolina was asked to furnish two regiments. It was following this call for troops that North Carolina seceded. Prior to this date the State had refused to leave the Union. North Carolina had been next to the last state to join the federal Union (November 21, 1789) and she was reluctant to leave.

The State was for the Union, but at the same time she did not feel she could wage war against her neighboring states of South Carolina, Virginia, and Tennessee as well as the other southern states whose economic and social life were more in accord with her own.

When North Carolina seceded she began immediately to prepare for war. General James G. Martin, adjutant general of the State, proceeded to organize and train volunteers as they joined the army. Also Martin began to purchase equipment and supplies for the soldiers. The State was rapidly developing an organized force for her defense. Manufacturing was greatly increased and supplies were purchased abroad. Many items were needed such as cannon, small arms, munitions, blankets, shoes, clothing, cotton and wool cards, salt, medicine, and many other items too numerous to mention. Not only the men of the State, but the women joined in the struggle for states' rights and southern independence.

The Federal forces, of course, began to prepare for war and troops were sent to subdue the South. So far as North Carolina was concerned, the eastern part of the State was the objective. Most of the fighting during the four-year period took place there. Roanoke Island, Morehead City, Beaufort, New Bern, and Washington fell into the hands of the Federal troops. Plymouth likewise was captured, recaptured, and later reoccupied by

Federal troops. North Carolina tried not only to defend her own territory, but at the same time sent troops to Virginia to join the Confederate forces in that and other theaters of operations. It was in 1864 that the Confederates recaptured Plymouth with the aid of the ironclad ram "Albemarle." Later the same year, after the "Albemarle" was torpedoed, the Federals recaptured the town. Fort Fisher fell to the Federals in 1865 and the final battle in the State took place at Bentonville, March 19, 20, and 21, 1865, when General W. T. Sherman's army coming up from the South met the army under General Joseph E. Johnston. Shortly after this battle, Johnston surrendered to Sherman near Durham and that ended the war in North Carolina except, of course, there were a few skirmishes here and there.

This very brief statement does not in any manner tell the story of this sectional conflict. It does attempt to record a few of the problems leading up to the war and to mention some of the towns which fell to the Federals during the War.

At the end of the conflict the State was bled white in men and resources. The State was occupied by Federal troops and the orderly process of government was practically nil. In fact, a new government was established. Following the collapse after the War, Reconstruction was inaugurated which lasted through 1868. It was not, however, until 1876 that a conservative government was voted into power and North Carolina, although exhausted from loss of man power and economic goods, began to return to a normal and routine life.

NORTH CAROLINA GOVERNORS

North Carolina had three governors during the War. John W. Ellis was governor when President Lincoln called for troops. Ellis replied immediately and among other things wired the President ". . . I regard a levy of troops for the purpose of subjugating the states of the South, as in violation of the Constitution and a usurpation of power.

"I can be no party to this wicked violation of the laws of the country, and to this war upon the liberties of the free people. You can get no troops from North Carolina."

John W. Ellis was born in Rowan County, November 23, 1820. His parents were Anderson and Judy Bailey Ellis. He attended Randolph-Macon College and graduated from the University of North Carolina, and later studied law under Judge Richmond M. Pearson. Ellis was a Democrat and an advocate of internal improvements; served in the House of Commons, 1844, 1846, and 1848; was elected judge of the Superior Court in 1848 and served until 1858 when he was elected governor; was re-elected governor in 1860 and served until July 7, 1861, when he died in office. He was succeeded by Henry T. Clark.

Henry T. Clark was born in Edgecombe County in 1808. He graduated from the University of North Carolina and later received an M.A. Degree. He was a farmer who became interested in politics; served in the State Senate from Edgecombe County, 1850 to 1860, and in 1866; was speaker of the Senate in 1858-1859 and 1860-1861. On June 27, 1861, the State Convention informed Clark of Governor Ellis' illness and he assumed the duties of governor. In July he officially succeeded Ellis who died July 7. Clark filled the unexpired term during which time he urged the State to maintain a force sufficient for its defense, but action by the Convention checked volunteering and a number of companies were not available when they were needed. Clark was considered a man of high character and commanded the respect of all parties. He did not seek election to suceed Ellis. He died April 14, 1874.

The next governor was Zebulon B. Vance who was elected in 1862. Vance was born May 13, 1830, in Buncombe County. He attended the University of North Carolina where he became a friend of David L. Swain, President of the University and also a native of Buncombe County. In 1854 Vance was elected to the House of Commons. In 1858 he was elected to Congress and took his seat on December 7; was re-elected in 1860; was a strong Union man until Lincoln called for 75,000 troops and North Carolina seceded from the Union. He organized the "Rough and Ready Guards" and was commissioned captain on May 5, 1861. Shortly thereafter he joined the Fourteenth Regiment under William D. Pender and saw service at Hatteras, New Bern, and the Seven Days Battle at Richmond. In August, 1861, he was elected colonel of the Twenty-Sixth Regiment. At first he refused to be a candidate for governor, but was prevailed upon to run and was elected in 1862 by a large majority. In fact his popularity was so great that he received every vote in his regiment. In 1864 he was again elected governor, but the war ended before the end of his term and he surrendered to General John M. Schofield. He was again elected governor in 1876, but resigned in 1879 to serve in the United States Senate to which he had been elected. He served there until his death in 1894.

CONFEDERATE CABINET MEMBERS

North Carolina furnished two members of President Jefferson Davis' cabinet. Both men had held important positions in the state or Confederate governments prior to or during the war. Thomas Bragg was Governor, 1855-1859, and United States Senator, 1860. George Davis served in the Confederate Congress—in the House 1861, and in the Senate 1862. Both men served as attorney general of the Confederate States of America.

Thomas Bragg (November 9, 1810-January 21, 1872) was born in Warrenton. He attended the academy in Warrenton after which he attended the military academy at Middletown, Connecticut. He studied law under Judge John Hall and began to practice in 1833 in Jackson, North Carolina. He served in the legislature, 1842; as governor, January 1, 1855, to January 1, 1859, and in the United States Senate, 1860, until the State seceded when he resigned. On November 21, 1861, he accepted the position of attorney general in President Davis' cabinet and served until March 18, 1862.

George Davis (March 1, 1820-February 23, 1896) was born on a farm in New Hanover County. He graduated from the University of North Carolina at the age of 18 with the highest honors and was licensed to practice law in 1840 but was not admitted to the bar until he reached his majority. He served in the Confederate House of Representatives in 1861 and in the Senate in 1862. On January 4, 1864, President Jefferson Davis invited him to become attorney general of the Confederate States, which position he held until the final dissolution of the Confederate government at Charlotte on April 26, 1865.

NORTH CAROLINA GENERALS

During the Civil War North Carolina furnished two lieutenant generals, six major generals, and twenty-five brigadier generals to the Confederacy. Some of the men were graduates of West Point and had had previous military experience. Theophilus H. Holmes and Daniel Harvey Hill come to mind. Hill, however, was a native of South Carolina but had made his home in North Carolina several years prior to the War. Some men had not had military training, but because of their bravery, their zeal for the Confederacy, and their ability to discipline and inspire men reached the rank of major general. Two of them were Bryan Grimes and Robert F. Hoke. The same is generally true of the brigadier generals. Junius Daniel, Richard C. Gatlin, Stephen D. Ramseur, James G. Martin, and others graduated from West Point while such brigadier generals as Rufus Barringer, Thomas L. Clingman, Robert B. Vance, Matt W. Ransom, James B. Gordon, and others were not West Pointers.

Of the six major generals, three were killed in battle or died from wounds. Stephen D. Ramseur served under a temporary commission—a practice which the Confederate government frequently followed. Six brigadier generals were killed in battle or died from wounds. Four brigadier generals received temporary appointments.

In addition to these men who were commissioned by the Confederate government, eight were commissioned brigadier generals by the State, four of whom served as adjutant generals—James G. Martin, Daniel G. Fowle, Richard C. Gatlin, and John F. Hoke.

Some natives of the State prior to the War had settled in other states and became high ranking officers there, such as the Forney brothers, one of whom graduated from West Point. Both men were in the Confederate army from Alabama. Robert Bullock, a native of Greenville, was living in Florida and served from that state. Leonidas Polk was a native of the State, but was living in the Southwest at the beginning of the War. He was a graduate of West Point, but after receiving his commission resigned from the army and entered the Episcopal ministry.

When the War began he volunteered for service and was appointed major, June 25, 1861, and was commissioned lieutenant general, October 10, 1862. Many other native North Carolinians could be listed.

Of course, all men were not generals. There were colonels, lieutenant colonels, majors, captains, lieutenants, and noncommissioned officers, as well as the common or private soldier. North Carolina furnished her part of the soldiers as well as the supplies. No definite number of men who were in the War is known, but it has been estimated that the State furnished approximately 125,000. In fact, before the War ended so many men and, in many instances, young boys in their teens were in the army or had been killed that Governor Vance said that the War was getting the "seed corn." North Carolinians gave their substance, their money, their efforts, and their blood in the cause which they believed was right and just. They were slow to leave the Union, but when the decision was reached they were ready to give their all—and many did.

Bryan Grimes (November 2, 1828-August 14, 1880) was born in Pitt County. He was graduated from the University of North Carolina in 1848. He was a large slave and plantation owner and a member of the Convention of 1861. In May, 1861, he was appointed major of the Fourth North Carolina Regiment and resigned from the Convention to take that assignment. On May 1, 1862, he was commissioned lieutenant colonel; on May 19, 1864, he was commissioned brigadier general; and on February 15, 1865, he was appointed major general. He was a good disciplinarian and distinguished for his bravery. During the War he had six horses shot from under him. Shortly after the War, he returned to his plantation near Grimesland and engaged in farming. Because of his efforts in the community to rid it of certain merchants, he was ambushed and shot near his home, and died August 14, 1880.

William Dorsey Pender (February 6, 1834-July 18, 1863) was born in Edgecombe County. He graduated from West Point in 1854. Upon graduating he was commissioned a second lieutenant in the First Artillery. In 1855 he was transferred to the First Dragoons and in 1858 was promoted first lieutenant. He saw active service in New Mexico, California, Oregon, and Washington. When the Civil War began he resigned from the United States Army and was commissioned captain of artillery and was placed in command of recruiting in Baltimore.

He returned to North Carolina in May, 1861, and on May 16 was elected colonel of the Third North Carolina Volunteers. On August 15 he was transferred to the Sixth North Carolina Regiment. Because of his brilliant leadership at Seven Pines he was promoted to brigadier general. On May 27, 1863, he was appointed major general. In July, 1863, he was at Gettysburg and was wounded on July 2. He was removed to Staunton, Virginia, where he died July 18, 1863, following an operation for the amputation of his leg. Pender County was named in his honor.

William Henry Chase Whiting (March 22, 1824-March 10, 1865) was a native of Mississippi. After graduating from Georgetown College (Washington, D. C.) with the highest honors attained up to that time, he entered West Point and was graduated in 1845. He engaged in river and harbor improvements and fortifications until he resigned February 20, 1861, having attained the rank of captain. He joined the Confederate Army and planned new defenses of Charleston Harbor and Morris Island. He later served in the Army of the Shenandoah, fought at First Bull Run and Seven Pines, and was appointed brigadier general August 28, 1861. In November, 1862, he took command of the military district of Wilmington, made the Cape Fear River a haven for blockade-runners, and developed Fort Fisher. He was promoted major general in February, 1863, and transferred to Petersburg but later returned to North Carolina at his own request, and aided Colonel William Lamb in defense of Fort Fisher where he was wounded January, 1865, and died on March 10, 1865.

Robert Ransom (February 12, 1828-January 14, 1892) was born in Warren County. He graduated from the United States Military Academy in 1850 and served on the frontier in Indian fighting and scouting. Later he taught cavalry tactics at West Point. At the beginning of the Civil War he resigned his commission and on May 24, 1861, was commissioned a captain in the Confederate Army. On October 13, 1861, he was commissioned colonel of the First North Carolina Regiment and appointed brigadier general on March 6, 1862. He fought in the Seven Days Battle and in June, 1862, was at Harpers Ferry and Antietam, and was promoted to major general May 26, 1863. He was relieved of his command in August, 1864, because of ill health. He surrendered to Howard at Warrenton, May 2, 1865. After the war he was express agent and city manager of Wilmington, 1866-1867; chairman of Railroad Supplies, 1868-1874; farmer, 1874-1878; and engineer in charge of river and harbor improvements in North and South Carolina until his death.

Daniel Harvey Hill (July 12, 1821-September 24, 1889) was a native of York District, South Carolina. He graduated from West Point in 1842 and participated in the Mexican War and was brevetted captain and later major. He resigned from the United States Army in 1849 to teach mathematics at Washington College, Lexington, Virginia. In 1854 he became professor of mathematics at Davidson College, and in 1859, was manager and commander of the Military Institute at Charlotte. When hostilities began he was invited to take charge of a company at Raleigh and was appointed colonel. On August 10, 1861, he was appointed brigadier general; and on March 26, 1862, was appointed major general; and on July 11 was appointed lieutenant general, but his promotion was not sent to the Confederate States Senate. He did, however, serve with that title until the end of the War.

Theophilus Hunter Holmes (November 13, 1804-June 21, 1880), was a native of Sampson County. He graduated from West Point in 1829. While serving in the United States Army he attained the rank of major and served in the Mexican War. On April 21, 1861, he resigned from the United States Army and cast his lot with the Confederacy. He was appointed brigadier general on June 5, 1861; major general, October 7, 1861; and lieutenant general to rank from October 10, 1862. He commanded a brigade at First Manassas and a division during the Seven Days Battle. Later he was transferred to the Trans-Mississippi Department from which position he finally relieved General Kirby Smith. He commanded the District of Arkansas for a time and later organized reserves in North Carolina. After the war he lived on a small farm near Fayetteville.

James Byron Gordon (November 21, 1822-May 18, 1864) was a native of Wilkes County. He attended Emory and Henry College, Emory, Virginia, and engaged in farming. He was a member of the House of Representatives in 1850. He enlisted as a volunteer in the Wilkes Valley Guards on May 9, 1861, and in August, became major of the First North Carolina Cavalry. Gordon served in the Virginia Theater of the War, and early in 1862 was transferred to North Carolina to meet Burnside at Kinston. He was promoted to lieutenant colonel April 3, 1863; and on June 29 he was ordered back to Virginia; in 1863 he was at Gettysburg. On September 28, 1863, he was commissioned brigadier general and assigned to the First Brigade of North Carolina Cavalry; was mortally wounded at Brooks Church on May 12, and died in Richmond May 18, 1864.

Thomas Lanier Clingman (July 27, 1812-November 3, 1897) was born in Huntsville. He graduated from the University of North Carolina in 1832, studied law, and was admitted to the bar in 1834. He served in the General Assembly in 1836 and 1840 and represented his district in Congress in 1843-1845 and 1847-1858. He resigned from the House of Representatives, May 7, 1858, to become a United States Senator. He resigned from the Senate, March 28, 1861, and in the fall of 1861 was commissioned colonel of the Twenty-fifth North Carolina Regiment. On May 17, 1862, he was commissioned brigadier general and participated in the battle around New Bern. He commanded a brigade at the Wilderness and fought at Drewy's Bluff and Cold Harbor, and was wounded twice, being able to return to his command only a few days before the surrender at Greensboro. After the War, he was active in politics. He explored the Great Smoky Mountains and developed the mica mines in that area. Clingman's Dome was named in his honor.

Lawrence O'Bryan Branch (November 28, 1820-September 17, 1862) was born in Halifax County. He graduated from Princeton University, studied law in Tennessee, and began to practice law in Florida. He participated in the Seminole War in 1841-1848. He moved to Raleigh and in 1855 was elected to Congress where he served until March 3, 1861. In April, 1861, he joined the Raleigh Rifles as a private and on May 20, was appointed to the office of paymaster and quartermaster general. In September he was commissioned colonel of the Thirty-third North Carolina Regiment and on November 16, 1861, President Davis appointed him brigadier general. His assignment was around New Bern but after the fall of New Bern he was transferred to Virginia. He participated in the Battle of Cedar Run, Second Manassas, Fairfax Courthouse, Harpers Ferry, and Sharpsburg (Antietam). While trying to get a better view of the Battle of Sharpsburg he was shot through the head and fell into the arms of Major Joseph Englehard, an officer attached to the staff, where he died.

Robert B. Vance (April 24, 1828-November 28, 1899) was a native of Buncombe County. He was a merchant and clerk of the Court of Pleas and Quarter Sessions. He organized and was captain of the Buncombe Rifle Guards which became part of the Twenty-ninth North Carolina Regiment, and was commissioned colonel in October, 1861, and the next month was sent to Eastern Tennessee to guard the railroad. He was next stationed at Cumberland Gap where he remained until June, 1862. While at Shiloh and Stone River he took over the Second Brigade when his commander was killed. While ill with typhoid fever, he was appointed brigadier general, April 23, 1863, which ranked from March 4. He was captured at Crosby Creek, Tennessee, January 14, 1865, and was paroled March 14, 1865. After the War, he served in the United States Congress, 1873 1885.

Rufus Barringer (December 2, 1821-February 3, 1895) was a native of Cabarrus County. He graduated from the University of North Carolina in 1842. At the beginning of the War, he raised a company of cavalry which became Company F of the First North Carolina Cavalry. On May 16, 1861, he was commissioned captain and on August 26, 1863, he was commissioned major, and three months later lieutenant colonel. He and James B. Gordon were in the same brigade and in June, 1864, after the death of Gordon, he was commissioned brigadier general, and was given command of the brigade. He was in 26 engagements, was wounded three times, and had two horses killed under him. On April 3, 1865, he was taken prisoner and detained at Fort Delaware until August, 1865. After the War, he engaged in the practice of law.

Collett Leventhorpe (May 15, 1815-December 1, 1889) was a native of Exmouth, Devonshire, England. He served in Her Majesty's Fourteenth Regiment of Foot, and for a number of years was on colonial duty. Later he immigrated to the United States and settled in North Carolina where he married. At the beginning of the War, he offered his services and was elected colonel of the Thirty-fourth North Carolina Regiment. He served in North Carolina with great credit. In 1863, his regiment joined the army in Northern Virginia and took part in the Battle of Gettysburg. He was wounded on the first day of battle and during the retreat fell into the hands of the enemy. When he was released nine months later, Governor Vance, in 1864, appointed him brigadier general of State troops. President Davis appointed him brigadier general in the Confederate service on February 3, 1865, and he was confirmed by the Confederate Senate, but declined the appointment on March 6, 1865. Some years after the War, he made his home in Wilkes County.

Two major generals of the Federal forces, one of whom operated in the eastern part and the other in the western of the State.

Ambrose Everett Burnside (May 23, 1824-September 3, 1881) was a native of Liberty, Indiana. He graduated from West Point in 1847 and served in Indian wars and in the Mexican War. In January, 1862, he sailed to Hatteras Inlet and in February captured Roanoke Island. In March, 1862, he occupied New Bern and in April laid siege to Fort Macon and Beaufort. He was commissioned a major general in 1862 and after the war resigned his commission and held important positions in railroad and other corporations. He was governor of Rhode Island, 1866-1869, and United States Senator, 1875-1881.

George Stoneman (August 8, 1822-September 5, 1894) was born in Chautauqua County, New York, and graduated from West Point in 1846. He was with the dragoons in Indian fighting and on the frontier and was a member of the Southwestern Expedition. He served in the Mexican War after which he was in command of Fort Brown, Texas. When the War began he was named major of the First United States Cavalry on May 9, 1861. He was transferred to the Fourth United States Cavalry on August 3, and ten days later was appointed brigadier general and commanded the cavalry reserves from August to October, 1861. From October, 1861, to January, 1862, he commanded the cavalry in the Army of the Potomac. Between January, 1862, and March 9, 1865, he held several commands and participated in several raids, including his raid into Western North Carolina from Tennessee. He retired as a colonel in 1871 and served as Democratic governor of California from 1883 to 1887.

THE PRIVATE SOLDIER AT WAR

There were more than 125,000 Tar Heels who fought for the Confederacy. They participated in almost every major battle during the four years of fighting. Because of their record they acquired the following "Rebel Boast":

First at Bethel
Farthest to the front at Gettysburg and at Chickamauga
Last at Appomattox.

A part of this legend is inscribed on the monument to the Confederate private soldier which faces west on Capitol Square in Raleigh.

The private soldier and noncommissioned officers represented every segment of the State's population. The German, Scotch-Irish, English, and Highland Scot elements were equally devoted to "The Cause" and all displayed the same gallantry, endurance, obedience, and bravery. North Carolina has every right to be proud of the long, grey lines which fought on every front. It is also true that the State had many deserters; but these were men who never wanted to take up arms for a fight in which they had no interest, economic or otherwise. In the following section the uniforms, weapons, camp life, and battles of the Confederacy are pictured. In so brief a study only the battlefields of North Carolina are shown. Most of these are drawings made by on-the-scene artists who followed the conflict on land and sea.

Henry Lawson Wyatt, who fell in the first victory at Bethel, is typical of the young and brave men who answered the call for troops. In no other state was the conscript act so well enforced, possibly accounting for the fact that this State suffered a greater loss of lives than any other in the South.

There are numerous letters from "rebel" Tar Heels in collections throughout the State. They are letters filled with details of the weather, of lice and "bugs" in camps and hospitals, of dreary marches and train rides without enough food, of horrible prisons and gory operations on the wounded, of foraging and pillaging, and of their love and respect, or dislike, of their leaders.

The State, through the efforts of Vance and his administration, was able to purchase enough woolen cloth for 250,000 uniforms, 12,000 overcoats, shoes and leather for shoes for 250,000 pairs, 50,000 blankets, and $50,000 gold value of medicines, and other supplies.

The record of North Carolina during the War Between the States is one which may be recalled with pride and satisfaction. Here, too, her men lived up to her motto: *Esse Quam Videri.*

Confederate soldier at Gettysburg, July 1, 2, and 3, 1863.

Confederate soldier, 1861-1865.

Confederate deserters in the mountains. *Pictorial War Record,* October
27, 1883.

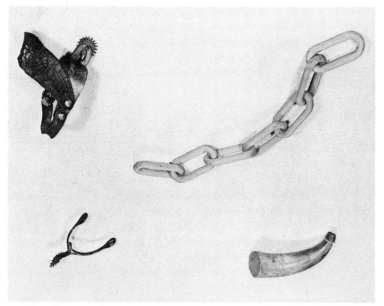

Top left and bottom are cavalry spurs used by General Robert Ransom, *top right* is chain carved by a Union soldier in the Salisbury Prison, and *bottom right* is a powder horn made from a cow horn used by Berry Carroll during the war. These items are in the Hall of History.

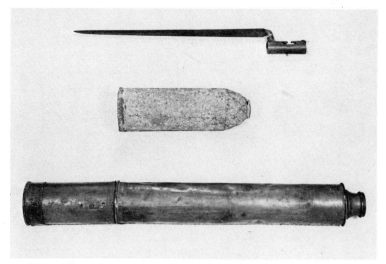

From *top to bottom*, bayonet used during the war, a three-inch Confederate shell fired at the Battle of Bentonville March 19-21, 1865, and spy glasses of James N. Craig used at Fort Fisher. These items are on display in the Hall of History.

Left to right: Canteen marked "L. L. Young" used during the Civil War. Young served in the Fifth Regiment, North Carolina Troops. Canteen carried by Corporal Samuel Commodore Kerley of Burke County, Company F, Forty-first Regiment. The skillet was used by a Confederate soldier. These items are housed in the Hall of History.

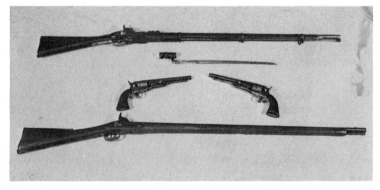

Top: 1862 Enfield Rifle and bayonet; *center:* 1860 Army Colts; *bottom:* Home-made Confederate musket. These were typical Confederate weapons and are housed in the Hall of History.

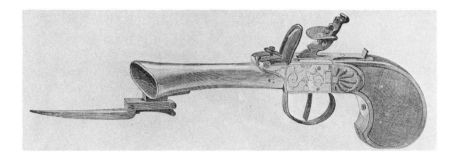

An old blunderbuss pistol captured from a Confederate during a raid into Maryland, May, 1863, is shown above. An officer of the First United States Cavalry under General George Stoneman took the pistol while his troops attacked the rear of General Lee's army. The pistol was of ancient construction with a brass barrel, bell muzzle, and depressed top and bottom. It had an old-fashioned flint lock, the spring of which was so firm only a strong finger could pull the trigger. Under the barrel was a spring bayonet, which when turned back was held in place by a guard. The stock was of very hard wood. The weapon was obviously of English manufacture. *Pictorial War Record* (page 389).

This type of gun, a 10-inch mortar, was used in the attack on Fort Macon.

This field piece is typical of the movable guns which were used during the War Between the States. *American Soldier in the Civil War* (page 286).

This type of gun was used at emplacements where mounted artillery was used for attack and defense. Guns like this were used at Fort Fisher and Fort Macon. *American Soldier in the Civil War* (page 75).

"A Holiday Scene—Confederate and Union Pickets Drinking a Merry Christmas and a Happy New Year," as sketched for the *Pictorial War Record* (pages 140-141). The men are enjoying give and take in the best of spirits, and they frequently used these opportunities to exchange articles of luxury and comfort, such as coffee or tobacco.

Edwin Forbes sketched this scene of army life, "Horseshoeing in the Army," for the *American Soldier in the Civil War* (page 312).

"A Night Burial on the Battlefield," depicts one of the most gruesome aspects of the Civil War. As soon as a battle was over, the troops usually retired from the field and the work of saving the wounded and burying the dead began. The surgeons and hospital corps, lanterns in hand, would scour the field for the wounded—friend and foe alike. Working with them were the parties detailed to bury the dead. The bodies of the dead were searched and articles removed to be sent home if possible. The officer in charge recorded the name and regiment and saw to burial in a shallow grave. Later the government had the soldiers disinterred and they were reburied in various national cemeteries. Sometimes a friend or body servant took a body home for burial in a family plot or church-yard. *American Soldier in the Civil War* (page 288).

"Fight at Hatteras Inlet Showing the Gunboat 'Monticello' Commanded by Lieutenant Braine." This battle occurred on October 5, 1861, and left the Confederate forces scattered along the shore for a distance of about four miles. *Pictorial War Record* (page 211).

"Death of O. Jennings Wise—Bringing Him Ashore After the Battle." One of the Confederates taken at Roanoke Island was this officer who was mortally wounded. The Union forces swarmed over the island, retrieving knapsacks, knives, guns, pistols, clothing, and food abandoned by the fleeing Confederates. *Pictorial War Record* (page 369).

The interior of Fort Bartow during the bombardment, February 7, 1862. *Frank Leslie's Illustrated Newspaper,* March 8, 1862.

An explosion of a cannon on board the gunboat "Hetzel" at Fort Bartow, Roanoke Island, February 7, 1862. Sketch by J. Bentley. *Pictorial War Record,* July 15, 1882.

A view of New Bern from the interior of Fort Thompson, after its capture by National Forces was drawn by artist Schell for *Frank Leslie's Illustrated Newspaper*, April 5, 1862. The smoke indicates the burning of the rosin works, the railway bridge, and naval stores. Vessels were sunk in the channel to prevent the approach of Federal gunboats.

Schell depicts the landing of Union troops under the orders of General Ambrose E. Burnside at Slocum's Creek at Neuse River, 15 miles below New Bern. From this point the troops attacked the Town of New Bern. *Frank Leslie's Illustrated Newspaper*, April 5, 1862.

Beaufort, showing Fort Macon in the distance, right of center. Notice the Confederate barque "Cecil" on fire, also the Confederate ships, "Alliance" and "Gondar" in the distance, left of center, and another ship on the extreme right. Drawing by Schell, artist for *Leslie's Illustrated Weekly*.

The capture of Fort Macon, April 26, 1862. Notice that the Confederate flag is being lowered on the flagpole. From a sketch by Schell, artist for *Leslie's Illustrated Weekly*.

The "Albemarle" afloat.

The ironclad "Albemarle" was built on the banks of the Roanoke River and participated in the recapture of Plymouth, April 17-20, 1864, when Confederate forces under General Robert F. Hoke attacked the Federal forces which had been holding Plymouth since it was captured by them December 13, 1862. On October 27, 1864, the Federals torpedoed and sank the "Albemarle."

The capture of Plymouth, October 31, 1864. From a drawing.

The war in New Bern. The view is from the opposite bank of the Neuse River. The drawing was made by an artist following General Burnside's army (April, 1862).

The scene above, taken from the *Pictorial War Record* (pages 380-381), shows the battle at New Bern on March 14, 1862, during which the Fourth Rhode Island Regiment captured a battery and rifle pits. They were assisted by the Fifth Rhode Island and the Eighth and Eleventh Connecticut regiments.

The Federal leaders realized by 1863 that Wilmington and Fort Fisher were vital not only to North Carolina but to the whole Confederacy, especially to Lee's troops in Virginia. Colonel William Lamb and General W. H. C. Whiting had joined in making this fort so strong it was referred to as "Gibraltar." It certainly afforded excellent protection to the blockade-runners with its Whitworth guns booming away at the Federal fleet when it came too close. From July 20, 1861, until January 15, 1865, the guns of this fort were active. Colonel William Lamb was a strikingly handsome man with dark wavy hair. He wore a slouch hat and his gray uniform had the longer coat affected by many officers, so that he made a dashing picture when booted. He also wore a holstered revolver and a sword. His wife, who was a native of the North, was called "Daisy" by her friends and was a great favorite of the pilots and captains of the blockade-runners.

During the Christmas holidays, 1864, the Federal fleet began to bombard the fort. On Christmas Day Union land forces drew near but did not attack as General Benjamin F. Butler thought that Fisher could not be taken. The fleet, under Admiral David D. Porter, sailed away but returned January 12, 1865, and aided by forces under General Alfred H. Terry began a determined attack. Complete surrender of the Confederate fort was made on January 15. Some of the most courageous hand-to-hand fighting of the entire war occurred during these three days. Tne above picture was taken from *Harper's Weekly*, February 4, 1865.

Sherman's troops marching from Savannah, Georgia, to Bentonville, North Carolina. An artist's drawing. This march has been described as "total war" because the troops destroyed as they marched.

Sherman's troops foraging on a plantation. Drawn by James E. Taylor, 1888. In addition to maintaining an army, Sherman's march was joined by hundreds of Negroes and many Union sympathizers.

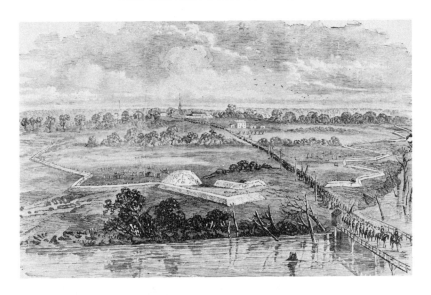

General John M. Schofield's army is shown leaving Wilmington, March, 1865, on its march to Goldsboro to meet Sherman. Confederate works which were behind the city can be seen. Schofield had assumed command and captured Wilmington on Washington's Birthday. He dispatched the Twenty-Third Corps via New Bern and on to Kinston where they met General Braxton Bragg's forces in severe battle on March 8. *Below,* Bragg retreated to Goldsboro with Schofield in hot pursuit. Both drawings are from the *American Soldier in the Civil War* (page 431).

E. F. Mullen sketched this scene of a Union official administering the oath of allegiance to Confederate prisoners for the *American Soldier in the Civil War* (page 312). General U. S. Grant allowed the captured soldiers of Lee's Army to take home their horses to help with the crops; military prisons were emptied but before the men could return home they had to swear allegiance to the conquering government. They were then sent home to begin a new way of life and to try to recover from four years of bitter struggle. Some of the generals like Robert E. Lee and North Carolina's Robert F. Hoke set examples by adjusting to civilian life during Reconstruction.

BLOCKADE-RUNNING

Fleet and beautiful were the especially designed and built vessels which slipped in and out of the ports along the Atlantic coastline to defy the blockading squadrons of the Union Navy. The blockade covered more than 3,500 miles with three main lines leading into Wilmington, from Halifax, Bermuda, and Nassau.

It was about 640 miles from the Bahamas to the two entrances to the Cape Fear River. Fort Fisher, "the Gibraltar of the Confederacy," guarded the entry at New Inlet; Forts Caswell and Campbell guarded the lower passage at Old Inlet. Colonel William Lamb held off the Union forces for almost three years and when Fort Fisher fell, January 15, 1865, the Confederacy was finished.

During the years when every ship carried a valuable cargo the chases were exciting and challenging. On many occasions agents, spies, and military personnel of the South were aboard and escape was imperative. Courage and speed were requisites but none of the converted ships were as fast as the blockade-runners made for the Confederacy in England and Scotland.

The crews were made up of dedicated southerners, veterans of the Royal Navy, and "packet rats" picked up in various ports. For risking their lives they received $100 monthly in gold and $50 bounty per trip—or about every seven days. The pilot, whose skill and daring were necessary to bring the runners "over the bar," received £700 to £800 sterling per round trip. Once safely out to sea the pilot could relax and relive the thrill of the chase. Late in 1862 a good pilot could demand $5,000 in gold per trip in addition to other concessions. More than 2,000 ships were brought safely into port in the Carolinas during the war years.

Silks, laces, and other finery for milady and rare wines for the gentlemen were brought in, but far more important were the loads of food, clothing, and gunpowder needed by the military. The blockade-runners brought medicines—opium, calomel, and quinine; spices and pepper, as well as tea and coffee, and fresh fruits. Surgical instruments were packed tightly in the holds along with imported toys for the children. The ships carried another precious cargo—mail—and with very few losses. These were the life line of the Confederacy—the orders and correspondence to and from the agents who tried so desperately to enlist support abroad.

When a ship was captured it was stripped and the captain and the crew were carried to a northern port where they were imprisoned and later exchanged. The pilots, however, were kept in prison as they were considered too dangerous to release.

During the blockade tea sold up to $500 per pound and a quarter of a lamb sold for $100. Confederate bills became so worthless that they were exchanged at the rate of $2,000 for one dollar of "hard money." Many captains refused to accept Confederate bills as payment.

Some of the most famous of the blockade-runners were the "Ad-Vance," bought by the State of North Carolina and captained by a Scotsman, Captain Willie (Wylie) ; the "R. E. Lee," which made more than 21 runs and carried cargoes worth a total of two million in gold; the "Hattie," making more than sixty trips; and the "Pet," a daring little steamer; the "Banshee," the "Lillian," and the "Florie," all of which made numerous runs. They were captained by John M. Maffitt, John Wilkinson, Louis M. Coxetter, Frank Bonneau, and others motivated by the gamble, the gold, or patriotism. The list of pilots is long, but these are some of those who were best known: C. C. Morse, George Thomas, and J. N. Burruss, Charles W. and T. W. Craig, R. S. and Thomas Grissom, and Henry Howard.

The wrecks of some of the runners lie bleaching in the sands of Carolina's shore, and the firing no longer echoes through the mist and spray—but the stories still thrill the hearts of those who like a chase—win or lose.

The North Carolina-owned steamer "Ad-Vance" made its first trip through the Atlantic blockade in the spring of 1863. Purchased in Scotland at the instigation of Governor Zebulon B. Vance, the vessel is said to have been named in his honor. It was commanded by Thomas M. Crossan and captained by a Scotsman named Wylie (also spelled Willie). The ship, originally called the "Lord Clyde," slipped in and out of the blockade with such regularity that its arrival could be calculated almost to the day. On January 20, 1864, she was grounded on the bar, but the batteries of Fort Fisher and Bald Head protected her until tugs and steamers released her to be towed up the river to safety. Another exciting run took place in July, 1864, when the "Ad-Vance" made the light at Cape Lookout instead of the light at Cape Fear. Under the battery of heavy Union guns and using inferior coal the ship finally rounded the shoal, or spit, and came under the protecting Whitworth guns of Colonel William Lamb at Fort Fisher. In September, 1864, on a trip out from Wilmington the "Ad-Vance" was captured. The firemen were having to use Chatham County coal, "or Egypt coal," as they had used their last shovel of good coal to cross the bar in full view of the Federal fleet of about thirty vessels. After the ship was taken it was converted by the Union and is said to have taken part in the second bombardment of Fort Fisher. It reappeared at the Cape Fear entrance in 1867 as a man-of-war called "Frolic."

The "Lilian" ("Lillian"), a British-built steamer, is shown running the blockade into Wilmington with John N. Maffitt as captain. Here Maffitt is shown watching the Union cruisers through binoculars. This sketch was drawn by Frank Vizetelly, who was a special artist for the *Illustrated London News*. Vizetelly originally followed the Union Army but transferred his interest to the South. He was often a guest of Colonel and Mrs. William Lamb near Fort Fisher where he fascinated them with the stories of his career as an artist in Paris during the time of Napoleon III and the Empress Eugenié.

The blockade-runner "Banshee" which was captured November 21, 1863. *Official Records of the Union and Confederate Navies in the War of the Rebellion*, IX, 318.

Fort Macon   "Nashville"   "State of Georgia"
                     Town of Beaufort

Sketched by artist E. Laurent for the *Pictorial War Record* (page 383) this scene shows the Confederate steamer "Nashville" running the blockade at Beaufort. In order to get into port the captain had the Stars and Stripes run up; when the "Nashville" was well into harbor, he hauled down the Union flag and sent up the Confederate "Bars." The steamer had been taken by the Confederates in Charleston, and made into a blockade-runner which had slipped through the South Carolina blockade.

The blockade-runner "Lady Davis"

THE HOME FRONT

While the men and boys of North Carolina fought at Manassas, New Bern, Richmond, Gettysburg, and elsewhere for the Confederacy, the people at home—women, children, and old men—were fighting a different kind of battle. Fought mostly without weapons, theirs was a bitter struggle and frequently the casualty lists were as great as those of the battlefield. Fevers and agues, hunger and measles were routine, and during one epidemic in Wilmington 2,500 died of "yellow jack." The War interrupted the educational program of Calvin H. Wiley; it disrupted transportation for civilians, but there were few places to go in the South; and changed a whole way of life for southerners. It wiped out older industries and started new ones vital to the South, such as the salt works at Morehead City and there were approximately fifty cotton mills in the State in 1861 which continued, with few exceptions, to work throughout the war years—some night and day. About one-half to three-fourths of the yarn and cloth produced was bought by the State and during the last few months of the War the Confederacy relied solely on the textile mills of our State.

At the Federal Arsenal in Fayetteville, which was captured by the order of Governor John W. Ellis on April 22, 1861, there were about 37,000 stand of arms valued at more than a quarter of a million dollars. The Salisbury Machine Works and the Cranberry Iron Works produced arms which placed North Carolina in an enviable position, or so it would seem. Not so! Generously the State gave Virginia 12,000 stand and equipped her own troops until September 19, 1861, when the Thirty-First North Carolina Regiment was formed. These men were forced to go out into the counties and find arms wherever they could, so that when they appeared at Roanoke Island they were poorly equipped. Two Frenchmen at Wilmington were employed to make sabers, swords, bayonets, and knives which were passed along to the troops as rapidly as they were completed. At Kenansville, in Duplin County, another factory produced similar products. Several gunsmiths in Guilford County, especially at Jamestown, were given a contract by General James G. Martin, chief of all the war departments in the State, to make 300 new rifles per month. About 10,000 rifles were received from these artisans making a total of 52,000 stand of arms placed in the hands of troops at the expense of the State. Many weapons were repaired and converted but there is no way to account for this work.

Not all of those at home were able to fire a forge or wield a hammer for the boys at the front. For many, day succeeded endless day with the drudgery of plowing, planting, and harvesting of crops—often to have it burned or taken by foragers or deserters. Women learned to plant and hoe, to make soap from ashes, to dye yarn, and to make homespun which they wore with pride. They wore out their shoes and made new ones, they dosed their children and the slaves that remained with roots and herbs, and wrote long letters to men who had thought when they left home that the War would "be over by fall." They parched corn, dried fig leaves and bark for tea and coffee, or when they had money paid the great price for items smuggled in; they went to church and fervently prayed for victory, then lay awake at night fearing slave revolts, "Buffalo" or Unionists attacks, and most of all that the Yankees would come. The Yankees did come—to the East and the West—and Tar Heels who had opposed secession gave them aid.

Though unwanted by the people of Salisbury a prison for captured Union soldiers was established there. Thousands of the enemy were enclosed here and were treated brutally. But this was War—war at its worst—and neighbor fought neighbor and brother fought brother.

Women served as agents and spies, they smuggled goods into the South, they nursed the sick and wounded in homes, churches, colleges, hospitals, or wherever they found them. They joined sewing circles, making "janes" and shirts which they sent to the camps, often folded around a tract, a testament, or a Bible.

It was not always dark and bleak, there was some singing and dancing. There were play parties with games and charades; there were holidays made festive with turkeys costing $250 and hams costing $175; and although goods could no longer be bought, gifts were improvised and "do-it-yourself" projects taxed the imagination of everyone.

Young boys and old men joined the Home Guard and fought the Unionists at home and the ever-encircling armies of the North, until the Federal forces conquered the State. When the smoke of battle cleared the South realized that war is fought, not with valor and spirit, but with supplies of cold steel and hot lead—and that peace is often won by surrender.

Older residents of Carteret County can identify the site of this "Rebel" salt works at Morehead City.

Common turpentine, once a leading product of the Tar Heel State, is obtained from pine trees. This sketch appeared in an 1858 issue of *Ballou's Pictorial Drawing-Room Companion* and shows the trees "boxed" and stripped. Pails are placed beneath the slashes to catch the honey-colored rosin which dripped from the cuts. A healthy pine might yield from six to twelve pounds annually. The South used turpentine as medicine during the war years.

Edwin Forbes drew this picture for *Harper's Weekly* (May 12, 1866) when cotton was no longer "king" in the South. Slave labor was utilized before the War, and during the War cotton was the gold of the Confederacy to be exchanged for necessities.

On February 13, 1864, this sketch by a Union prisoner was published in *Frank Leslie's Illustrated Newspaper* and entitled "Money Crisis in the South—Auction Sale of a Five Dollar Gold Piece at Danville, Near the North Carolina Border." After spirited bidding the gold piece was "knocked down for $150 Confederate money."

Patriotic southern women sewed for "the Cause" and urged their beaux to volunteer. From I. T. Trowbridge's, *A Picture of the Desolated States* (page 188).

The most expert smugglers during the War were women. Here a southern woman is unloading boots which she attempted to carry through Union lines. *Pictorial War Record* (page 3).

After the Emancipation Proclamation there were many runaway slaves. Slave-owners and other southerners organized search parties and attempted to return them to their homes. This drawing in the *Pictorial War Record* (page 3) shows the artist's idea of how they were abused when recaptured.

This sketch illustrates a scene in the South where ignorant secession farmers assassinated their neighbors who were loyal to the Union. This was often done in the presence of the victim's family. The attackers then took all of the food and livestock and left the survivors destitute. Cruelties of this kind became less frequent as the War progressed. *Pictorial War Record* (page 218).

Homemade shuck hat, bottle, and shoe with wooden sole made during the war. These items are on display in the Hall of History.

Spinning and weaving equipment. *Left to right,* click wheel, flax wheel, and flax break. On the floor are three flax hackles. These items are on display in the Hall of History.

THE FREEDMEN

Jubilation and shouts of joy over the gift of freedom swept through the ranks of 350,000 former slaves in North Carolina. They were "freedmen" at last; drunk with this unaccustomed emotion many gathered their scant belongings and fled to nearby towns or other states. Some were soon to be in jails, to be hungry and sick, as well as homeless. They were taking part in a social revolution of which they had been the cause and were both the victor and the victim.

Tar Heels who had fought for "The Cause" limped home from the vermin-infested camps and prisons to mend their houses, their barns, and their fences, and in some instances to pull their plows. Approximately 40,000 North Carolinians did not come back, many of them lying in unknown graves. Like other slaveholders, their investment in the more than $200,000,000 in slaves in the South was a total loss. They suffered the loss of other uncounted millions of dollars in property and economic collapse seemed inevitable. There were from North Carolina 23,000 men and over 400 officers who had deserted the armies of the Confederacy; they came from hiding in the swamps and mountain coves to help rebuild their State.

There was stamina left in the people of the State, however, and they faced the political and social upheaval with determination. Farms became more numerous with less acreage as the share-cropping plan replaced the plantation system of farming.

Although Tar Heels as a whole resented the Freedmen's Bureau, and although it was undoubtedly infiltrated with a few scoundrels, much good was accomplished by this agency. More than $1,500,000 worth of food was distributed, 40,000 patients were cared for and hospitals were opened, 431 schools for freedmen with 439 teachers for over 20,000 pupils were started by the Bureau.

The marriages of former slaves were validated, they were given equal rights and privileges in courts of law and equity, and measures were enacted to safeguard them from being defrauded.

There were problems to come: North Carolina was to serve a long and bitter sentence for her reluctant secession from the Union. Obstacles to be overcome included military occupation by United States troops, the problems involved in readmission to the Union, the invasion of carpetbaggers, the expensive ($100,-000) Constitutional Convention of 1868, the rise of the Union League and the Ku Klux Klan, the sordid fraud involving graft and waste at every level of government, and the bankruptcy of private and public funds.

The impoverished State reeled under the blows engendered by surrender and oncoming Reconstruction, but the freedmen had no thought of this. With light hearts they were able to shout, "Freedom!"

A runaway slave is shown hiding in the swamp while a friend from a neighboring plantation brings him food. His own family would not feed him as that might lead to his capture. These runaways tried to reach the Union lines where they often gave valuable information to the enemy. *Pictorial War Record* (page 206).

Many women of the North volunteered to go South and teach the freedmen. Adults and children alike attended the classes. This artist's sketch appeared in J. T. Trowbridge's *A Picture of the Desolated States* (page 388).

After President Lincoln issued the Emancipation Proclamation, September 23, 1862, which became effective January 1, 1863, many slaves fled to towns and areas under the control of Federal troops. The drawing published in *Harper's Weekly*, February 21, 1863, shows the effects of the proclamation.

Many Negroes went to New Bern after that town had been captured by Federal troops. These Negroes were settled on the Trent River. Generals Stedman and Fullerton are conferring with the Negroes in a church in the settlement. This is a drawing by Theodore R. Davis.

Theodore Davis sketched these drawings of the Trent River settlement at New Bern for *Harper's Weekly*, June 9, 1866. The top picture shows a negro hut, the schoolhouse and chapel are shown in the center sketch, and the bottom picture shows the "squatters" walking home along the tracks, while one Negro fishes in the river.

Along with his freedom, the Negro was given many rights heretofore denied him. One of these was the privilege of voting in political elections. Here an orator exhorts his fellows to participate, punctuating his remarks with his umbrella.

"Turning the Tables on the Overseer" was the universal dream of the slaves. They could conceive no more brutal treatment than whipping with a lash. This unsigned picture shows the overseer stripped to the waist and a slave ready with the whip.

"The Lessee" reflects the daydream of an elderly slave who has become a lessee (tenant) on the plantation he once worked before emancipation.

Younger and more ambitious this young contraband fancies himself in the uniform of the "Government." His idea is to protect and defend his race as they enter a new phase of southern life.

Here the artist shows the jubilant Negroes in a sketch, "Pay Day on the Plantation." In their daydream they are receiving *money* for their labor with the right to spend it as they please.

NORTH CAROLINA REMEMBERS HER SACRIFICES

North Carolina Memorial at Gettysburg, Military
Park, Pennsylvania, erected by the State honoring
her soldiers in the battle which took place there
July 1, 2, and 3, 1863. The Twenty-sixth North
Carolina Regiment suffered a greater loss of dead
and wounded than any regiment participating in
the battle. In 1927 and 1929 the General Assembly
appropriated a total of $50,000 for a memorial, and
Gutzon Borglum was employed as the sculptor. On
July 3, 1929, the memorial was unveiled. Governor
O. Max Gardner made a brief address and former
Governor Angus W. McLean delivered the principal
address. Major General B. F. Cheatham accepted it.

SOME BOOKS ABOUT THE CIVIL WAR

Ammen, Daniel. *The Atlantic Coast.* New York: C. Scribner's Sons, 1883.

Anderson, Mrs. John H. *North Carolina Women of the Confederacy.* Fayetteville: Cumberland Printing Company for the Author, 1926.

Arthur, John Preston. *Western North Carolina: A History (From 1730 to 1913).* Raleigh: Edwards and Broughton Printing Company, 1914.

Ashe, Samuel A'Court. *History of North Carolina.* Volume II. Raleigh: Edwards and Broughton Printing Co., 1925.

Barrett, John G. *The Civil War in North Carolina.* Chapel Hill: University of North Carolina Press, 1963.

——————. *Sherman's March through the Carolinas.* Chapel Hill: University of North Carolina Press, 1956.

Clark, Walter, ed. *Histories of the Several Regiments and Battalions from North Carolina in the Great War, 1861-'65.* Raleigh: E. M. Uzzell, 5 volumes, 1901.

Connor, Robert D. W. *North Carolina: Rebuilding an Ancient Commonwealth, 1584-1925.* Volume II. Chicago: American Historical Society, Inc., 1929.

Crabtree, Beth G., and James W. Patton, eds. *"Journal of a Secesh Lady": The Diary of Catherine Ann Devereux Edmondston, 1860-1866.* Raleigh: Division of Archives and History, North Carolina Department of Cultural Resources, 1979.

Dykeman, Wilma. *The French Broad.* New York: Rinehart and Co., 1955.

Hamilton, J. G. de Roulhac. *Reconstruction in North Carolina.* New York: Columbia University, 1914.

Hill, Daniel Harvey. *North Carolina in the War Between the States—Bethel to Sharpsburg.* Raleigh: Edwards and Broughton Printing Co., 2 volumes, 1926.

——————. *North Carolina* (Volume IV of *Confederate Military History*, edited by C. A. Evans). Atlanta: Confederate Publishing Co., 1899.

Johnson, Robert U., and Clarence C. Buel, eds. *Battles and Leaders of the Civil War.* New York: Century Co., 4 volumes, 1888.

Manarin, Louis H., and Weymouth T. Jordan, Jr., eds. *North Carolina Troops, 1861-1865: A Roster.* Raleigh: Division of Archives and History, North Carolina Department of Cultural Resources, projected multivolume series, 1966—.

Massachusetts Memorial to Her Soldiers and Sailors Who Died in the Department of North Carolina, 1861-1865. Boston: Gardner and Taplin, 1909.

Operations on the Atlantic Coast, 1861-1865, Virginia, 1862, 1864, Vicksburg . . . (Volume IX of *Papers of the Military Historical Society of Massachusetts*). Boston: Military Historical Society of Massachusetts, 1912.

Sitterson, Joseph Carlyle. *The Secession Movement in North Carolina.* Chapel Hill: University of North Carolina Press, 1939.

Sloan, John A. *North Carolina in the War Between the States.* Washington: Rufus H. Darby, 1883.

Spencer, Cornelia Phillips. *The Last Ninety Days of the War in North Carolina.* New York: Watchman Publishing Co., 1866.

Sprunt, James. *Chronicles of the Cape Fear River, Being Some Account of Historic Events on the Cape Fear River.* Raleigh: Edwards and Broughton Printing Co., 1914.

Stick, David. *The Outer Banks of North Carolina.* Chapel Hill: University of North Carolina Press, 1958.

Tatum, Georgia L. *Disloyalty in the Confederacy.* Chapel Hill: University of North Carolina Press, 1934.

Waddell, Alfred M. *The Last Year of the War in North Carolina, Including Plymouth, Fort Fisher, and Bentonsville.* Richmond: W. E. Jones, 1888.

Yates, Richard E. *The Confederacy and Zeb Vance* (Volume VIII of *Confederate Centennial Studies*, edited by William S. Hoole). Tuscaloosa, Alabama: Confederate Publishing Co., 1958.